FOR KIDS

Cutie Pies

FOR KIDS

Jennifer Adams

PHOTOGRAPHS BY ZAC WILLIAMS

GIBBS SMITH
TO ENRICH AND INSPIRE HUMANKIND

Manufactured in Shenzhen, China, in June 2011 by Toppan

The cooking and baking activities suggested in this book may involve the use of sharp objects and hot surfaces. Parental guidance is recommended. The author and publisher disclaim all responsibility for injury resulting from the performance of any activities listed in this book. Readers assume all legal responsibility for their actions.

First Edition
15 14 13 12 11   5 4 3 2 1

Published by
Gibbs Smith
P.O. Box 667
Layton, Utah 84041

1.800.835.4993 orders
www.gibbs-smith.com

Designed by Sheryl Dickert Smith

Gibbs Smith books are printed on either recycled, 100% post-consumer waste, FSC-certified papers or on paper produced from sustainable PEFC-certified forest/controlled wood source. Learn more at www.pefc.org.

Library of Congress Cataloging-in-Publication Data

Adams, Jennifer.
  Cutie pies for kids / Jennifer Adams ; photographs by Zac Williams. — 1st ed.
     p. cm.
  ISBN 978-1-4236-2049-5
  1. Pies. 2. Cookbooks. I. Title.
  TX773.A324 2011
  641.8'652—dc22
                        2011001926

Contents

HEY CUTIE! · 6

Hey Cutie!

Pies are a friendly dessert. They are easy to make and fun to eat. Mini pies are especially fun because you and your friends each get your very own pie for yourself!

Officially, a pie is a pastry crust filled with fruit, cream, or other filling. Pies traditionally have a top pastry crust covering the filling. In this book, a pie is loosely defined as a sweet dessert having a crust and a filling of some sort. You'll find creamy pies, fruity pies, frozen pies, and extreme pies. This book will teach you to make crusts from graham cracker crumbs and cookie crumbs, as well as regular homemade piecrusts. Readymade piecrusts, such as those found in the refrigerated section of your grocery store, are a great timesaving option and produce delicious pies.

Mini Pie Pans

The pie tins used for the mini pies in this book are Wilton 4¾-inch mini

tart/quiche pans with removable bottoms. They are available in a set of 6 and are the perfect size for these recipes.

If you choose to purchase premade graham cracker crusts for mini pies at the grocery store, or if you want to make your mini pies in large muffin pans, you will need to reduce

the amount of filling per pie so the filling doesn't run over. This also means you can make 1 or 2 more pies from the same recipe. An adult who has baking experience can help you make these adjustments.

WHOLE PIES

Almost all recipes in this book make 8 mini pies. Almost all recipes can be made as 1 whole pie instead. Generally speaking, there are only a couple of changes. On recipes with baked crusts, the baking time will need to be increased. On recipes that need to set in the refrigerator or freezer, the time should be doubled. As long as you watch this—especially your baking times—you should be able to make a large pie if you want.

A NOTE ON INGREDIENTS

Use butter, not margarine. For pudding, use 2 percent milk. Skim milk or low-fat milk will not give good results. Soy milk will not work. In most cases, use whipped cream, not frozen whipped topping.

WHIPPED CREAM AND VARIATIONS

Many of the recipes in this book call for whipped cream. Here is a simple recipe. There are also several variations for flavored whipped creams if you want to dress up your pie recipes.

Whipped Cream

    1 pint whipping cream
    1 teaspoon vanilla extract
    ¼ cup powdered sugar
       or more to taste

To make whipped cream, be sure the cream, bowl, and beaters are chilled. Whip cream on high speed until soft peaks form. Add vanilla and powdered sugar and continue beating until somewhat stiff peaks form.

Cinnamon-Spice Whipped Cream

    1 cup whipping cream
  1-2 tablespoons powdered sugar
    1 teaspoon ground cinnamon
    ½ teaspoon ground nutmeg

Follow instructions for Whipped Cream, adding sugar and spices after soft peaks form.

Salted Caramel Whipped Cream

- 1 cup whipping cream
- ¼ teaspoon salt
- 1 tablespoon caramel sauce

Follow instructions for Whipped Cream, adding salt and caramel after soft peaks form.

HOMEMADE PIECRUSTS

- 1 cup cold unsalted butter, cut in pieces
- 2½ cups all-purpose flour
- 1 teaspoon salt
- 1 teaspoon sugar
- 6–8 tablespoons ice water

Cut the butter into ½-inch cubes and place in the freezer for 15 minutes to 1 hour.

Combine the flour, salt, and sugar using a pastry cutter or a food processor. Cut in the butter or pulse until the mixture is in small crumbs the size of peas. Add ice water, 1 tablespoon at a time, until mixture just begins to clump together. Pinch a piece of the crumbly dough between your fingers. If it holds together, it's ready. If it doesn't, add another tablespoon of water. Continue until dough holds together.

Place dough in a mound on a clean surface. Divide in half and shape into 2 rounds. Knead dough just enough to form into rounds, but do not overknead or it will be hard to roll. You will be able to see little bits of butter in the dough. Sprinkle with flour and wrap each round in plastic wrap. Refrigerate at least 1 hour or overnight.

Two-Crust Pies

Remove one round of dough from the refrigerator and let sit at room temperature for 5 to 10 minutes. Using a rolling pin, roll out dough on a lightly floured surface into a 12-inch circle, about 1/8 inch thick.

Cut out dough in circles slightly larger than the mini pie pans you are filling. Gently press dough down so it lines the bottoms and sides of pans. Trim excess dough to within 1/2 inch or less of the edge of the pans. Add filling.

Roll out the second round of dough, as you did the first. Wet the edge of the crust with a little bit of water on your finger. Then place circles of dough on top of filled pies. Press top and bottom rounds together.

Flute the edges (to look like a ruffle) by pinching the dough between your thumb and forefinger every half inch or so. Or you can decorate the edge of the crust by pressing around the outside edge with a fork. Cut a couple of slits in the tops of piecrusts to allow steam to escape during baking.

Prebaked Crust

If you are making a prebaked crust, line the bottom and sides of pans with dough. Flute the edges and poke holes in the bottom with a fork so the crust doesn't bubble up while baking. Put dough-lined mini pie pans on a sheet pan and bake on a rack in the middle of the oven at 350 degrees F for 10 to 15 minutes, or until crusts are golden. Remove crusts from oven and cool completely before filling.

Graham Cracker Crust

2 cups graham cracker crumbs

½ cup sugar

½ cup butter, melted

Mix together graham cracker crumbs, sugar, and butter. Press into the bottoms and sides of mini pie pans.

Oreo Crumb Crust

2 cups Oreo cookie crumbs

½ cup sugar

½ cup butter, melted

Mix together Oreo crumbs, sugar, and butter. Press into the bottoms and sides of mini pie pans.

TOPPINGS AND GARNISHES

A topping or garnish can turn a regular pie into a super fun one. Most of the recipes in this book include garnishes, from chopped cookies to candy canes to fresh berries to fortune cookies. When making these recipes, think of other edible treats to garnish your pies. Be creative and have fun!

Monkeys Go Bananas!

1 recipe Oreo crumb crust (page 10)

1 large package banana cream instant pudding mix

3 cups milk (2 percent)

Whipped cream

Runts candy bananas

Press about ¼ cup Oreo crumb crust into the bottom and sides of 8 mini pie pans or muffin pans fitted with paper liners.

In a bowl, mix together pudding mix and milk. Whisk for 3 to 5 minutes while pudding thickens.

Pour banana pudding into prepared crusts. Place in the fridge to set for at least 1 hour.

Before serving, top each pie with whipped cream. Garnish with Runts candy bananas.

Makes 8 mini pies

Circus Peanut Butter Cup

FOR CRUST

½ cup butter, melted

1 cup graham cracker crumbs

1 cup powdered sugar

½ cup peanut butter

FOR PIE

1 large package chocolate instant pudding mix

3 cups milk (2 percent)

Whipped cream

Reese's Pieces

In a medium bowl, mix together butter, graham cracker crumbs, powdered sugar, and peanut butter until well blended. Divide evenly and pat into the bottoms of 8 mini pie pans or muffin pans fitted with paper liners.

In a bowl, mix together pudding mix and milk. Whisk for 3 to 5 minutes while pudding thickens.

Pour chocolate pudding into prepared crusts in mini pie pans. Place in the fridge to set for at least 1 hour.

To serve, top each pie with a dollop of whipped cream. Sprinkle with Reese's Pieces.

Makes 8 mini pies

Mini Mini Chocolate Chip

1 recipe homemade
   or readymade
   piecrust (page 8)

1 large package chocolate
   instant pudding mix

3 cups milk (2 percent)

Whipped cream

Mini chocolate chips

Fit 8 mini pie pans or other mini ovenproof molds with piecrust and bake according to directions. Set aside to cool.

In a bowl, mix together pudding mix and milk. Whisk for 3 to 5 minutes while pudding thickens.

Pour chocolate pudding into prepared crusts in mini pie pans. Place in the fridge to set for at least 1 hour.

To serve, top each pie with whipped cream and garnish with mini chocolate chips.

Makes 8 mini pies

Beach-Style Lemonade

FOR CRUST

- 2 cups Nilla wafer crumbs
- 4 tablespoons butter, melted

FOR PIE

- 1 can (21 ounces) Wilderness lemon pie filling
- 2 cups whipped cream

Thin lemon slices

To make crust, combine wafer crumbs and butter in a medium bowl. Press into the bottoms and sides of 12 mini pie pans or paper cupcake liners and chill for at least 2 hours before filling.

In a large bowl, fold together lemon pie filling and whipped cream. Spoon creamy lemon filling into prepared mini pie pans. Garnish with lemon slices.

Makes 12 mini pies

Asian Dragon Gingersnap

FOR CRUST

2 cups crushed gingersnap cookie crumbs

½ cup butter, melted

1 teaspoon grated orange zest

FOR PIE

2 small packages white chocolate instant pudding mix

3½ cups cold milk (2 percent)

8 fortune cookies

Orange zest

To make crust, combine cookie crumbs, butter, and orange zest in a medium bowl. Press into the bottoms and sides of 8 mini pie pans.

Make pudding according to package directions. Pour into prepared crusts in mini pie pans. Refrigerate at least 1 hour. When ready to serve, garnish each pie with a fortune cookie and a long curl of orange zest.

Makes 8 mini pies

Pirate's Limey

1 recipe graham cracker crust (page 10)

3 cups sweetened condensed milk

½ cup sour cream

¾ cup lime juice

Whipped cream

Crushed Jolly Rancher candies

Press crust into the bottoms and sides of 8 mini pie pans.

In a medium bowl, combine sweetened condensed milk, sour cream, and lime juice; mix well. Pour into prepared crusts.

Bake at 350 degrees F for only about 5 minutes, until tiny bubbles break on the top of the pies. Do not brown. Remove pies from oven and cool. Refrigerate 2 hours. Top each pie with whipped cream and decorate with candies.

Makes 8 mini pies

Very Blueberry

1 recipe homemade or readymade piecrust (page 8)

1 can (21 ounces) Wilderness blueberry pie filling

Preheat oven to 350 degrees F. Fit 8 mini pie pans with bottom crusts. Fill each to the top with pie filling. Cut a small star shape out of the center of each top crust using a mini cookie cutter, or cut freehand. Fit pies with top crusts and flute (crimp or pinch) the edges together.

Place pies on a baking sheet. Bake for approximately 30 minutes, or until crust is golden and filling is hot and bubbly. Cool before serving.

Makes 8 mini pies

Strawberry Kisses

FOR CRUST

1 package purchased
   sugar cookie dough

FOR FILLING

2 pints fresh strawberries

1 cup sugar

3 tablespoons cornstarch

¼ cup strawberry gelatin
   mix (½ small package)

1 cup boiling water

Whipped cream

Decorating sprinkles

Roll out dough to ½ inch thick and cut into 12 or more cookies with a heart-shaped cookie cutter. Bake according to package directions or until cookies are lightly brown at the edges. Let cool.

Wash strawberries and remove green tops. Slice each berry into 4 pieces. Set aside in a bowl.

In a saucepan, mix together the sugar, cornstarch, and gelatin until well blended. Add boiling water. Cook over medium heat, stirring with a long-handled spoon, until mixture thickens. Remove from heat and let cool to room temperature.

Drizzle the gelatin mixture into the strawberries and gently stir to coat the berries. Place a spoonful of strawberries onto each heart cookie. Chill in the refrigerator for at least 2 hours. Top with whipped cream and sprinkles before serving.

Makes 12 mini pies

Cran-Cherry

1 recipe homemade or readymade piecrust (page 8)

1 can (21 ounces) Wilderness cherry pie filling

1 cup fresh or frozen cranberries

½ cup sugar

Decorative white sugar crystals

Preheat oven to 350 degrees F. Fit 8 mini pie pans with bottom crusts. Slice top crusts into strips ½ inch thick. Cut out decorative shapes from extra crust.

In a large bowl, mix together cherry pie filling, cranberries, and sugar. Pour mixture into prepared pie pans.

Make a woven pattern with the top crust strips, laying them on top of the filled pies. Cut off ends that overhang edges of the pans. Press decorative crust shapes into white sugar crystals and arrange on top of filled pies.

Place pies on a baking sheet. Bake for approximately 30 minutes, or until crusts are golden brown and fruit is hot and bubbly. Cool before serving.

Makes 8 mini pies

Fruity Tartlets

FOR CRUST

6 tablespoons butter, softened

3 tablespoons sugar

¼ cup flour

1½ cups sliced almonds, pulsed briefly in a food processor

½ teaspoon almond extract

FOR TOPPING

1 package (4 ounces) cream cheese, softened

2 tablespoons powdered sugar

2 tablespoons milk (2 percent) or cream

Mandarin orange slices

Fresh raspberries

Fresh mint sprigs

Cream together butter and sugar. Add flour, almonds, and almond extract. Press into the bottoms only of 8 mini pie pans. Place pans on a baking sheet and bake at 400 degrees F for 8 to 10 minutes, or until edges are golden brown. Remove from oven, cool, and then chill in the refrigerator.

In a medium bowl, beat cream cheese with powdered sugar and milk or cream until smooth. Spread evenly over baked tartlet crusts. Arrange fruit on top of filling and garnish with mint before serving.

Makes 8 tartlets

Country Caramel Apple Crumble

FOR CRUST

- 1 recipe homemade or readymade piecrust (page 8)

Vanilla ice cream or Salted Caramel Whipped Cream (page 8) for serving

FOR TOPPING

- ¼ cup brown sugar
- ¼ cup flour
- 1 teaspoon cinnamon
- 2 tablespoons butter
- ½ cup chopped walnuts (optional)

FOR PIE

- 6 tart apples, peeled, cored, and diced
- 2 teaspoons lemon juice
- ½ cup sour cream

Preheat oven to 350 degrees F. Fit 8 mini pie pans with a bottom crust. Place pans on a baking sheet.

Mix together brown sugar, flour, and cinnamon. Cut in butter until crumbly. Add walnuts if using. Set aside.

Toss apples in lemon juice and stir in sour cream. Place apple filling into prepared crusts. Top each with some of the crumble topping. Bake for 30 to 40 minutes, until apples are tender. Serve warm with vanilla ice cream or Salted Caramel Whipped Cream.

Makes 8 mini pies

Peachy Keen

FOR CRUST

1 recipe homemade or readymade piecrust (page 8)

FOR TOPPING

1 cup sugar

Dash of salt

3 tablespoons cornstarch

¼ teaspoon nutmeg, plus more for garnish

1 teaspoon lemon zest

1 cup boiling water

4 cups pitted, peeled, and diced fresh peaches

Whipped cream or Cinnamon-Spice Whipped Cream (page 7)

Fit 8 mini pie pans with bottom crusts and place on a baking sheet. Bake at 350 degrees F for 8 to 10 minutes, or until golden brown at edges. Remove from oven and set aside to cool.

In a saucepan, mix together sugar, salt, cornstarch, nutmeg, and lemon zest until well blended. Add boiling water and, using a long-handled spoon, stir over medium heat until mixture thickens. Remove from heat and cool slightly.

Fill each baked piecrust with peaches and pour filling mixture over the top. Refrigerate for at least 2 hours. Serve topped with a dollop of whipped cream or Cinnamon-Spice Whipped Cream and a sprinkle of nutmeg.

Makes 8 mini pies

Four-and-Twenty Blackbirds

1 recipe homemade
   or readymade
   piecrust (page 8)

1 package (4 ounces)
   cream cheese, softened

2 tablespoons
   powdered sugar

4 tablespoons milk
   (2 percent) or
   cream, divided

1 can (21 ounces)
   Wilderness blackberry
   pie filling

Decorative white
   sugar crystals

Cut out 12 (4- to 5-inch) circles from the piecrust with a cookie cutter or biscuit cutter dipped in flour.

In a medium bowl, beat cream cheese with powdered sugar and 2 tablespoons milk or cream until smooth.

To assemble pies, spread 1 teaspoon of cream cheese mixture on one half of each piecrust circle. Top with 1 tablespoon of blackberry pie filling. Fold in half to make a mini fruit turnover and crimp edges together.

Place on a baking sheet that has been sprayed with nonstick cooking spray. Brush with milk or cream and sprinkle with sugar crystals. Bake at 350 degrees F for 20 to 30 minutes, or until golden brown.

Makes 12 mini handheld pies

Construction Cookie Dough

1 recipe graham cracker crust (page 10)

1 pint Ben and Jerry's Chocolate Chip Cookie Dough ice cream, softened

Whipped cream

Semisweet mini chocolate chips

Press about $1/4$ cup graham cracker crumb crust in the bottoms and sides of 8 mini pie pans.

Fill each piecrust with softened ice cream and smooth the tops. Arrange pie pans on a baking sheet and place in the freezer to refreeze, about 1 hour.

When ready to serve, remove from freezer and soften slightly. Top each mini pie with whipped cream and sprinkle with mini chocolate chips.

Makes 8 mini pies

Candy Cane Lane

1 recipe Oreo crumb crust (page 10)

1 pint peppermint ice cream, softened

1½ cups whipped cream

3 tablespoons crushed candy canes or peppermint candies

¼ cup semisweet mini chocolate chips

Mini candy canes, peppermint candies, and peppermint sticks

Press about ¼ cup Oreo crumb crust in the bottoms and sides of 8 mini pie pans. Set aside.

Place softened ice cream in a large bowl. Fold in whipped cream. Fold in crushed candy canes and mini chocolate chips. Mound into prepared mini pie pans. Place on a baking sheet and freeze for 2 hours, or until firm. To serve, soften slightly and garnish each mini pie with a mini candy cane, peppermint candy, or peppermint stick.

Makes 8 mini pies

Somethin' Fishy

1 recipe graham cracker crust (page 10)*

1 pint lime sherbet, softened

1 container (8 ounces) frozen whipped topping, thawed

Chocolate and Graham Cracker Goldfish

Press about ¼ cup crumb crust in the bottoms and sides of 8 mini pie pans or other small glass dishes. Set aside.

Mix Goldfish into softened sherbet. Fill each piecrust with sherbet and smooth the tops. Arrange pie pans on a baking sheet and place in the freezer to refreeze, about 2 hours. Remove from freezer and cover each pie with whipped topping. Return to freezer and freeze until whipped topping is frozen, about 2 more hours.

* You could make the crust using vanilla wafers.

Makes 8 mini pies

Garden Grasshopper

FOR CRUST

- 2 cups crushed Keebler Grasshopper cookies
- ¼ cup butter, melted

FOR PIE

- 1 jar (7 ounces) marshmallow creme
- 1 container (8 ounces) frozen whipped topping, thawed and divided
- 1 teaspoon mint extract
- 4 to 6 drops green food coloring
- 10 Keebler Grasshopper cookies, chopped

Green decorating sprinkles

In a medium bowl, mix together cookie crumbs and butter until well combined. Press about ¼ cup crumbs into the bottoms and sides of 8 mini pie pans. Place mini pans on a baking sheet and place in refrigerator to set crusts, about 1 hour.

In a large bowl, beat together marshmallow creme and 2 cups whipped topping until well blended. Stir in mint extract and food coloring. Fold in chopped cookies. Spoon filling into prepared mini pie pans and freeze for at least 4 hours. Pie will be firm, but not frozen solid. Top with remaining whipped topping and decorating sprinkles before serving.

Makes 8 mini pies

Too Too Berry

1 graham cracker crust (page 10)

3 containers (6 ounces each) raspberry yogurt

1 container (8 ounces) frozen whipped topping, thawed

1 cup fresh raspberries, plus more for garnish

Press about $1/4$ cup graham cracker crumb crust in the bottoms and sides of 8 mini pie pans.

In a large bowl, fold yogurt into whipped topping. Gently fold in 1 cup fresh raspberries. Spoon into prepared piecrusts and freeze for at least 2 hours.

When ready to serve, thaw for at least 15 minutes, then garnish with fresh raspberries.

Makes 8 mini pies

Gooey Swamp

FOR CRUST

- 1 cup graham cracker crumbs
- ½ cup butter, melted
- 1 cup semisweet chocolate chips
- 1 cup sweetened flaked coconut
- 1 cup chopped walnuts
- 1 can (14 ounces) sweetened condensed milk

FOR PIE

- 1 large package chocolate instant pudding mix
- 3 cups cold milk (2 percent)
- Whipped cream
- Gummy frogs

Mix together graham cracker crumbs and melted butter. Press into the bottoms and sides of 12 mini pie pans. Sprinkle an even amount of chocolate chips over each mini piecrust. Then sprinkle coconut, then nuts. Drizzle each with sweetened condensed milk. Bake at 350 degrees F for 20 minutes. Cool for at least 1 hour.

Make pudding according to package directions. Spoon chocolate pudding over prepared crusts in mini pie pans. Place in the fridge to set for at least 1 hour.

To serve, top each pie with whipped cream and a gummy frog.

Makes 12 mini pies

Jack-o-Lantern

1 recipe homemade or readymade piecrust (page 8)

1 package (8 ounces) cream cheese

½ cup powdered sugar

¾ cup sugar

½ teaspoon salt

1 teaspoon ground cinnamon

¼ teaspoon ground ginger

¼ teaspoon ground cloves

2 eggs

1 can (15 ounces) pumpkin

1 can (12 ounces) evaporated milk

Candy pumpkins

Fit the bottoms and sides of 12 mini pie pans or mini muffin pans with piecrust.

In a small bowl, cream together cream cheese and powdered sugar. Set aside.

In another small bowl, combine sugar, salt, cinnamon, ginger, and cloves. In a large bowl, slightly beat eggs. Stir in pumpkin and sugar-and-spice mixture. Stir in evaporated milk gradually.

Place prepared mini pie pans on baking sheets. Carefully spread 1 tablespoon cream cheese mixture as the bottom layer in each prepared crust. Pour pumpkin mixture over the top. Do not overfill, since the pumpkin puffs up when it cooks. Discard any extra filling.

Bake for 15 minutes at 425 degrees F. Reduce temperature to 350 degrees F and bake for an additional 20 minutes, or until a knife inserted in the center comes out clean. When pies are done, remove from oven and cool for 2 hours. Top each pie with a pumpkin candy.

Makes 12 mini pies

Little Critters Pecan

1 recipe homemade or readymade piecrust (page 8)

3 eggs

½ cup sugar

1 cup light corn syrup

½ teaspoon salt

1 teaspoon vanilla

¼ cup butter, melted

⅛ cup evaporated milk

1½ cups roughly chopped pecans

Fit the bottoms and sides of 8 mini pie pans with piecrust. Place on a baking sheet and set aside.

In a large bowl, slightly beat the eggs and add the sugar, corn syrup, and salt. Stir in vanilla, butter, evaporated milk, and pecans.

Pour pecan mixture into prepared mini pie pans and bake at 350 degrees F for 30 to 40 minutes, or until centers are set. Serve cool or slightly warm.

Makes 8 mini pies

S'more, Please

1 recipe graham cracker crust (page 10)

1 large package chocolate instant pudding mix

3 cups cold milk (2 percent)

1 bag (10.5 ounces) mini marshmallows

Press about ¼ cup graham cracker crumb crust into the bottoms and sides of 8 mini pie pans. Place pans on a baking sheet.

Make pudding according to package directions. Pour pudding into prepared crusts in mini pie pans. Top each with mini marshmallows. Place in the fridge to set for at least 1 hour.

Put oven on broil. Place baking sheet in oven and broil for just a minute or two, until tops of marshmallows are toasted. Serve immediately.

Makes 8 mini pies

Safari Toffee Brownie

1 packaged brownie mix

1 large package chocolate instant pudding mix

3 cups cold milk (2 percent)

Whipped cream

2 Heath candy bars, crushed

Prepare brownie batter according to package directions. Fit a muffin tin with decorative liners. Spread a little brownie mix, about $^1/_8$ to $^1/_4$ cup, evenly in the bottoms of muffin cups. Place muffin tin on a baking sheet and bake at 350 degrees F for 15 to 20 minutes, or until a toothpick inserted in the brownies comes out clean. Let cool.

Make pudding according to package directions. Pour pudding over prepared crusts. Place in the fridge to set for at least 1 hour.

To serve, top with whipped cream and sprinkle with crushed candy bars. Serve mini pies in the decorative liners.

Makes 12 mini pies

Chocolate Satin and Ribbons

FOR CRUST

- 1 cup lightly toasted and chopped hazelnuts
- ½ cup sugar
- 4 tablespoons butter, melted

FOR PIE

- 1 can (12 ounces) evaporated milk
- 2 egg yolks
- 2 cups semisweet chocolate chips

Whipped cream

Fresh raspberries for garnish

Hershey syrup for garnish

To toast nuts, place them in a pie pan and bake for 5 to 10 minutes at 350 degrees F. They will brown slightly. Remove from oven and let cool before touching.

Put the hazelnuts and sugar in a food processor and pulse for a few seconds. When combined, add butter and pulse a few seconds more. Press mixture into the bottoms and sides of 8 mini pie pans and set aside.

In a medium saucepan, whisk together evaporated milk and egg yolks. Heat over medium-low heat, stirring constantly, until mixture thickens slightly. Do not allow mixture to come to a boil. Remove from heat and stir in chocolate chips until completely melted and smooth.

Pour chocolate filling into prepared crusts and refrigerate for 2 hours, or until firm. Top each mini pie with a dollop of whipped cream and a raspberry. Drizzle Hershey syrup in ribbons over the tops.

Makes 8 mini pies

Alien Invasion Pistachio

FOR CRUST

1   cup flour

½   cup chopped walnuts

½   cup butter, melted

FOR PIE

1   package (8 ounces) cream cheese

½   cup powdered sugar

1   cup frozen whipped topping, thawed

1   small package pistachio instant pudding

2   cups cold milk (2 percent)

24 sour apple Dum Dum Pops

Black decorating gel

Green decorating sprinkles

To make crust, mix flour, walnuts, and butter together. Divide evenly and press into the bottoms only of 8 mini pie pans. Bake at 350 degrees F for 8 to 10 minutes. Let cool.

In a medium bowl, cream together cream cheese and powdered sugar. Stir in 1 cup of the whipped topping. Divide evenly and spread over the prepared piecrusts.

Make pudding according to package directions. Pour over the cream cheese layer in mini pie pans. Place in the fridge to set for at least 1 hour.

Draw alien eyes on each Dum Dum Pop using black decorating gel. Insert 3 alien pops into each mini pie and top with sprinkles.

Makes 8 mini pies

Whoopie Pies

FOR CRUSTS

- 1 package devil's
  food cake mix

FOR FILLING

- ½ cup shortening
- 1¼ cups powdered sugar
- 2 cups marshmallow creme
- 1 teaspoon vanilla

Prepare cake mix as directed on package, except use only ¾ cup of water. Drop batter in 3-inch circles onto a cookie sheet that has been sprayed with nonstick cooking spray. Bake at 350 degrees F for about 12 minutes, or until a toothpick inserted in the center comes out clean. Remove from oven and let cool.

To make the filling, beat together shortening and powdered sugar until creamy. Fold in marshmallow creme, then add vanilla. To assemble pies, turn over a cookie and spoon a dollop of filling onto the bottom of the cookie. Top with a second cookie, placing the bottom of the cookie on the filling. Press together.

Makes 12 whoopie pies

For my Aunt Alison,
from her favorite Cutie Pie

With special thanks to:

Lemon Meringue Anita Wood

Fresh Peach Charley Adams

Cream Cheese Kellie Robles

Pumpkin Linda Adams

Satin and Ribbons Madge Baird

Key Lime Melissa Dymock

Cherry Rhubarb Michelle Branson

Coconut Cream Nate Adams

Banana Cream Renee Bond

French Apple Sheryl Dickert Smith

Ryan's Apple Suzanne Taylor

Pecan Zac Williams